GLACIER PARK
AF407900

Glacier Park NICKnames
'BACKBONE OF the WORLD' - BLACKFEET NATION
'CROWN OF the CONTINENT' - GEORGE GRINNELL
'the AMERICAN ALPS' - GREAT NORTHERN RAILWAY
1

2

WHITE-TAILED PTARMIGAN FACTS

PLUMAGE IS WHITE IN THE WINTER →

+ BROWN IN THE SUMMER

THE SMALLEST OF THE GROUSE family

CAN BE SEEN ON LOGAN PASS IN GLACIER PARK

ORCHID FACTS

- OVER 20 SPECIES in GLACIER PARK.

- SOME SPECIES ARE as SMALL AS A DIME.

- 1 of the OLDEST FAMILIES OF FLOWERS.

- TAKES 5-7 YEARS TO BLOOM ONCE GERMINATED.

the FIRST U.S. PRESIDENT TO VISIT GLACIER PARK was FRANKLIN ROOSEVELT WHO DELIVERED A NATIONAL ADDRESS FROM EAST GLACIER.

5

DURING 1910

- GLACIER PARK WAS FORMED.

hailey's COMET WAS SEEN FROM EARTH.

THE WORLD'S FIRST PUBLIC RADIO BROADCAST WAS AIRED.

the FIRST FILM ADAPTATION OF FRANKENSTEIN WAS in THEATERS.

BUILT in 1928, the GLACIER PARK LODGE HAS THE 1st GOLF COURSE in MONTANA TO HAVE GRASS GREENS.

7

BEARGRASS isn't a grass nor eaten by bears. It is a common plant found in Glacier Park and has mass blooms every 5-10 years.

8

GLACIER PARK'S 1ST DEADLY BEAR ATTACKS
AKA NIGHT OF THE GRIZZLIES
IN 2 SEPARATE INCIDENTS ON THE SAME NIGHT IN 1967, 2 CAMPERS WERE FATALLY MAULED BY GRIZZLY BEARS IN GLACIER PARK.
9

AT 6,647 FT., _logan_ PASS is the HiGHEST POiNT in GLACiER PARK ACCESSiBLE BY VEHiCLE."

the
PTARMIGAN
TUNNEL is A
250 FOOT LONG
PEDESTRIAN SCALED
TUNNEL CUT THROUGH
A MOUNTAIN in
GLACIER PARK.
11

GLACIER PARK'S library HAS OVER 7000 BOOKS, PERIODICALS + DOCUMENTS ABOUT GLACIER PARK MADE AVAILABLE FOR the PUBLIC.
12

PROJECT SAFE SLIDE

In 1997, the National Park Service used sonic **booms** from jets to create controlled avalanches in Glacier Park.

13

the **PIEGAN** or Piikáni **IS** the **PRIMARY BAND** of the **BLACK FEET** nation who inhabited the AREA THAT is now GLACIER PARK.

EVEN WITH equipment THAT CAN MOVE 4000 tons OF SNOW PER HOUR, GLACIER PARK'S GOING to the SUN ROAD TAKES
10 WEEKS to PLOW.

15

BIRD WOMAN FALLS IS A 560FT WATERFALL WEST OF the continental DIVIDE IN GLACIER PARK. IT IS FED BY SNOWFIELDS + A REMNANT GLACIER.
WOW
16

A 46 MILLION YEAR OLD FOSSIL OF A MOSQUITO ENGORGED W/ BLOOD WAS FOUND IN A RIVER BED IN GLACIER PARK.

17

BROWNING, MT
is A TOWN NEAR GLACIER PARK + WAS the SETTING FOR THE X-FILES TV EPISODE: 'SHAPES' WHICH WAS INSPIRED BY the NATIVE AMERICAN LEGEND 'MANITOU'.

PIKA FACTS

- SMALLEST MEMBER OF THE RABBIT FAMILY.
- FOUND IN GLACIER PARK'S ALPINE TERRAIN.
- DOESN'T HIBERNATE.
- SENSITIVE TO TEMPS ABOVE 78°

19

AT THE ENTRANCE OF THE BLACK FEET RESERVATION, EAST OF GLACIER PARK, SITS 2 WARRIORS SCULPTED FROM the REMNANTS OF A 1964 FLOOD DISASTER.

GLACIER PARK'S 1ST ESSENTIAL BOOK WAS SELF-PUBLISHED IN 1924 BY MORTON ELROD. 'ELROD'S GUIDE' IS A COMPENDIUM OF maps, DESCRIPTIONS + PHOTOS OF GLACIER PARK.

21

hoary
MARMOT
FACTS
• KNOWN AS THE
'WHISTLE PIG'
FOR ITS HIGH PITCHED
ALARM CALL.
• HOARY REFERS to
ITS SILVER HAIR.
• CAN BE SEEN
ON LOGAN PASS
IN GLACIER PARK.

MOUNTAIN GOATS, AN icon OF GLACIER PARK AREN'T TRUE GOATS. they WERE MIS- NAMED FOR THEIR RESEMBLANCE to the DOMESTIC FARM ANIMAL.

NICKNAMED 'TRICK FALLS';
RUNNING EAGLE FALLS IN GLACIER PARK LOOKS LIKE 1 WATER-FALL, but IS ACTUALLY 2 WATERFALLS.
WATER-FALL 1
WATER-FALL 2
24

the LITTLE ICE AGE WAS A PERIOD OF BITTER WINTERS + MILD SUMMERS THAT MADE GLACIER PARK'S GLACIERS GROW to THEIR MAXIMUM SIZES.

the RECORD WIND GUST SPEED FOR GLACIER PARK is 139 MPH AND OCCURRED on LOGAN PASS.

26

GLACIER PARK lodge WAS CONSTRUCTED WITH WOOD FROM WESTERN AND EASTERN UNITED STATES + CONSIDERED TO BE A SYMBOL OF THE NATION'S COASTS JOINED.

27

the NORTH AMERICAN CONTINENTAL DIVIDE IS AN ELEVATED area that SEPARATES THE CONTINENT'S RIVER SYSTEMS + RUNS 106 MILES THROUGH GLACIER PARK.

the BLACKFEET NAME FOR RISING wolf MOUNTAIN IN GLACIER PARK is MAHKYU-OPUAHSIN, WHICH TRANSLATES to: THE WAY THE WOLF GETS UP.

ONE of the CAUSES OF AMPHIBIAN DIE offs IN GLACIER PARK is a SKIN FUNGUS, WHICH is SPREAD FROM HUMAN AQUATIC GEAR.

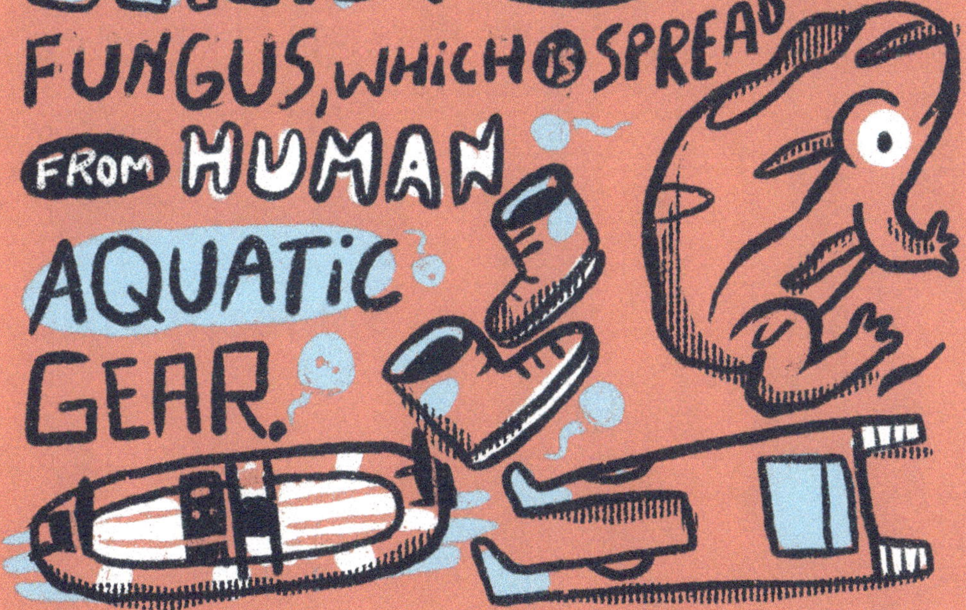

John 2 GUNS
WHITECALF
WAS A PIEGAN
BLACKfeet
CHIEF,
GLACIER PARK
CELEBRITY
AND RUMORED to be the
MODEL FOR THE ENGRAVED PROFILE
ON THE BUFFALO NICKEL.
LIBERTY
1913

31

FORMER GLACIER PARK ART SCHOOL STUDENT Gerald TAILFEATHERS WAS ONE OF THE 1ST indigenous CANADIANS to BECOME A PROFESSIONAL PAINTER.
1925-1975

in 1924 2 BROTHERS, JOSEPH + WILLIAM WHITEHEAD VANISHED WITHOUT A TRACE ON A HIKE from GRANITE PARK to LAKE MCDONALD IN GLACIER PARK.

33

GLACIER PARK has
little LIGHT POLLUTION
AND IS A CERTIFIED
DARK SKY PARK.
34

GEOLOGISTS CALL GLACIER PARK'S chief MOUNTAIN, A KLIPP, WHICH IS A BUTTE exposed BY EROSION W/DIFFERENT AGED ROCK LAYERS.

DIVERS at the BOTTOM OF LAKE Mcdonald IN GLACIER PARK have PROPPED UP FOUND TOOLS VERTICALLY FORMING A tool GARDEN.

36

the WEEPING WALL in GLACiER PARK is A ROCKFACE w/ CASCADING SPRING water ON THE GOING to the SUN ROAD.
ROLL UP THE WINDOW

the SEE AMERICA FIRST CAMPAIGN PROMOTED GLACIER PARK AS A VACATION ALTERNATIVE to EUROPE.

AN ABANDONED MINING TOWN in GLACIER PARK named ATLYN, was BURIED UNDERwater BY LAKE SHERBONE in 1921.

TRANSPORTING VISITORS SINCE 1936, the RED JAMMER tour BUSES in GLACIER PARK ARE PAINTED RED AND make A JAMMING SOUND WHEN SHIFTING.
JAM! JAM!

ALMOST every YEAR SINCE 1932, AMERICANS IN GLACIER PARK SHAKE hands OVER THE BORDER w/ CANADIANS in WATERTON PARK TO COMMEMORATE the FIRST international PEACE PARK.

41

ONE OF THE RUNNING SCENES FROM the 1994 FILM FORREST GUMP, SHOWS FORREST ON A BRIDGE IN GLACIER PARK.

42

in 1926
BRITISH MOUNTAINEER
DOROTHY PILLEY
RICHARDS SCALED
25 GLACIER
PARK PEAKS
in 19 DAYS.

43

BAT FACTS

GLACIER PARK HAS 9 BAT SPECIES.

BABY BATS ARE CALLED PUPS.

CAN CONSUME THEIR BODY WEIGHT IN INSECTS IN 1 NIGHT.

ONLY MAMMAL that CAN FLY.

GLACIER PARK'S LARGEST LAKE, LAKE MCDONALD, is RUMORED TO BE NAMED AFTER A FUR trapper WHO CARVED his NAME' ON A NEARBY TREE IN 1878.
MCDONALD

45

GLACIER PARK'S european STYLE CHALETS + ALP LIKE MOUNTAINS MADE IT KNOWN AS AMERICA'S SWITZERLAND.

46

WHITEBARK PINES IN GLACIER PARK STABILIZE SLOPES, PROVIDE FOOD + SHELTER TO WILDLIFE + SUSTAIN SNOW DRIFTS.
47

GLACIER PARK is losing its GLACIERS.
1890
150 GLACIERS
1968
83 GLACIERS
2021
25 GLACIERS
2030
0 GLACIERS

48

COVERED in SUMMER WILD FLOWERS, the GARDEN WALL is a POPULAR HIGHLINE trail in GLACIER PARK.

49

the OPENING SHOT OF ACCLAIMED horror MOVIE 'THE SHINING' WAS filmed IN GLACIER PARK.

WOLVERINE AKA SKUNK BEAR
FACTS
[CAN BE SEEN IN ALPINE AREAS OF GLACIER PARK]
LARGEST MEMBER OF THE WEASEL FAMILY
POOR VISION
STRONG SENSE OF SMELL
EMITS BAD ODORS
SOLO LIFE-STYLE
WATER-PROOF FUR
51

the SiNOPAH is
A 45 FT. LONG boat THAT
HAS TOURED GLACIER PARK'S
LAKES for 100+ YEARS.

WILD GOOSE island IS A 'TINY island THAT RISES ONLY 14 FEET ABOVE the SURFACE OF St. MARY'S LAKE in GLACIER PARK.

53

CHIEF
EARL OLD PERSON
WAS born NEAR GLACIER PARK AND SERVED THE LONGEST TERM AS A tribal OFFICIAL IN THE united STATES.

54

NAMES <u>OF THE</u> 9 SWISS CHALETS BUILT in GLACIER PARK BETWEEN 1910 + 1915:

LOUIS hill, A RAILROAD EXECUTIVE, HELPED to PROMOTE + ESTABLISH GLACIER PARK.

Elouise COBELL WAS BORN EAST OF GLACIER PARK + RECEIVED THE PRESIDENTIAL MEDAL OF FREEDOM for HER ACTIVISM ON BEHALF OF NATIVE AMERICANS.
1945-2011

57

BELLS were ONCE ATOP
of GLACIER PARK
PASSES for HiKERS
TO RiNG.
58

GLACIER PARK HAS shallow CANYONS FORMED BY MOVING glaciers OVER LARGER CANYONS CALLED HANGING VALLEYS.

59

MANY GLACIER HOTEL

in GLACIER PARK was NICKNAMED

SHOWPLACE OF THE ROCKIES

FOR ENTERTAINING GUESTS WITH *live* THEATER + MUSICALS.

STROMATOLITES
ARE 1.45 BILLION
year OLD FOSSILIZED
ALGAE, LOCATED
mainly AT HIGH
ELEVATIONS
ON THE
EASTSIDE
OF GLACIER
PARK.
61

long BEFORE WHITE EXPLORERS, NATIVE americans LIVED in THE AREA that is NOW GLACIER PARK.

EAST GLACIER
BLACK FEET
SALISH
WEST GLACIER
PEND d'ORIELLE
KOOTENAI

the TOP CAUSES OF DEATH in GLACIER PARK ARE:
1 DROWNING
2 VEHICLE ACCIDENT
3 CLIMBING FALL
4 HIKING FALL
5 heart ATTACK
63

OF GLACIER PARK'S 175 MOUNTAINS, 6 ARE ABOVE 10,000' FT. in Elevation.

JACKSON

MERRITT

KINTLA

CLEVELAND

STIMSON

SYEH

64

LOGAN PASS is
TYPICALLY 10-15 DEGREES
COLDER than LOWER ELEVATIONS
iN GLACIER
PARK.

65

there ARE THOUGHT TO BE
6-8 WOLF PACKS
IN GLACIER PARK.

66

POLEBRIDGE is A TOWN OF 100 NEAR GLACIER PARK and is POWERED by A DIESEL ENGINE and SOLAR PANELS.

PART of A NATIONAL PARK SERIES, GLACIER PARK'S 1ST POSTAGE stamp was RELEASED IN 1934.

68

3 trails in GLACIER PARK ARE WHEELCHAIR ACCESSIBLE:
1 SWIFTCURRENT TRAIL
2 trail OF THE CEDARS
3 RUNNING EAGLE FALLS trail

69

NO FISHING license IS REQUIRED to FISH within GLACIER PARK'S BOUNDARIES.
70

iN 1954 the GREAT NORTHERN RAILWAY sold its GRANITE PARK CHALETS to GLACIER PARK FOR $1.

71

the STRIKING COLORS OF GLACIER PARK'S lake ROCKS ARE DETERMINED BY THE PRESENCE OR ABSENCE OF IRON.

the LOOP is A HAIRPIN turn ON THE
GOING TO THE SUN ROAD,
IN GLACIER PARK.

73

an EDIBLE FLOWER IN GLACIER PARK CALLED fireweed CAN BE FOUND IN FOREST FIRE REMNANTS.
SOME FIREWEED TREATS:
74

FOUND ONLY in GLACIER PARK
the WESTERN GLACIER STONE FLY is AT RISK OF EXTINCTION DUE to LOSS OF SNOW-FIELD HABITAT.

GLACIER PARK hotel WAS DESIGNED AFTER PORTLAND, OREGON'S FORESTRY BUILDING, WHICH WAS ALSO CALLED 'the WORLD'S LARGEST log CABIN'.

named NINAISTAKO BY THE BLACKFEET tribe, CHIEF MOUNTAIN IN GLACIER PARK was USED FOR CEREMONIES FOR THOUSANDS OF YEARS.

BEAVER FACTS

REPTILES IN GLACIER PARK

GLACIER PARK (HAS
2 types OF GLACIERS.
1. ICE GLACIER: large MASSES OF COMPRESSED ice + SNOW.
2. ROCK GLACIER: LARGE MASSES OF ROCKS ice + MUD.

INSPIRED by GLACIER PARK'S BEAUTY, MONTANA ARTIST C.M. RUSSELL OWNED A CABIN + STUDIO ON LAKE McDONALD.
81

FACED with local
DISCRIMINATION +
DANGEROUS CONDITIONS
AFRICAN AMERICAN
SOLDIERS FOUGHT
GLACIER PARK
WILDFIRES
DURING THE
BIG BURN
OF 1910.

THE DUSTY STAR OBSERVATORY in GLACIER PARK POSTS A TIME-LAPSE VIDEO OF the PREVIOUS NIGHT SKY EVERY MORNING.

83

"FRANK" GUARDIPEE
was the FIRST
GLACIER
PARK
RANGER
from the
BLACK-
FEET
tribe.
84

the BIG DRIFT is A 50 FT. DEEP SNOW DRIFT that SEASONALLY COVERS A MILE OF THE GOING to the SUN ROAD in GLACIER PARK.

20% of MONTANA's
LOONS LIVE in
GLACIER PARK.
86

GREAT northern RAILWAY's
GLACIER PARK iNSPiRED
GOAT MASCOT
AND LOGO
was NAMED
ROCKY.

According to A 2019 STUDY,
THERE ARE 300 GRIZZLY BEARS in GLACIER PARK.
88

'there is no HIGHWAY which will give THE SEER, the LOVER OF GRANDEUR OF THE CREATOR'S handiwork, MORE THRILLS, MORE GENUINE SATISFACTION.. THAN A TRIP OVER THIS ROAD.'
- MT GOV. FRANK COONEY 
* GOING TO THE SUN ROAD, GLACIER PARK
89

GIVEN the NAME "NET-CHI-TA-KI" (LONE WOMAN) BY THE BLACKFEET tribe, ARTIST ELIZABETH LOCHRIE PAINTED MANY PORTRAITS OF THEIR PEOPLE IN GLACIER PARK.

BELT ☐ SUPER GROUP, AN ASSEMBLAGE OF 4.65 BILLION YEAR OLD SEDIMENTARY + IGNEOUS ROCKS.

OF GLACIER PARK'S (17) ORIGINAL lookouts, 9 remain AND ONLY (4) ARE in SERVICE DURING FIRE SEASON.

GLACIER PARK lakes ARE TURQUOISE FROM MELTING SNOW + GLACIAL SILT.
93

NICKNAMED WATERMELON SNOW for its PINK tint, SNOW ALGAE CAN BE SEEN IN GLACIER PARK GROWING ON FREEZING WATER.

94

the 4 ZONES OF GLACIER PARK

1. DEVELOPED ZONE

2. RUSTIC ZONE

3. BACK-COUNTRY ZONE

4. DAY USE ZONE

95

the TRIPLE DIVIDE PEAK IN GLACIER PARK is the HEADWATERS OF THE PACIFIC, ATLANTIC + ARCTIC OCEANS.

96

montana's 1st
oil well was
on the shores
of Kintla
lake in Glacier,
park.
97

IN 1969,
5 young
MOUNTAINEERS
WERE KILLED
by AN
AVALANCHE
on GLACIER
PARK'S MOUNT
CLEVELAND.

GEORGE BIRD GRINNELL
WAS A CONSERVATIONIST WHOSE EXPLORATIONS, WRITINGS AND POLITICAL ties HELPED ESTABLISH GLACIER PARK in 1910.

99

THE CIVILIAN CONSERVATION CORPS WAS A WORK RELIEF PROGRAM THAT GAVE YOUNG MEN EMPLOYMENT DURING THE GREAT DEPRESSION AND HELPED TO CREATE THE INFRA-STRUCTURE FOR GLACIER PARK.

100

DURING WINTER, VISITORS CAN SKI, HIKE OR SNOW-SHOE ON CLOSED ROADS IN GLACIER PARK.
101

HUCKLEBERRY

FACTS!

PICKING SEASON in GLACIER PARK BEGINS in AUGUST.

OFFICIAL STATE FRUIT of IDAHO. (MONTANA DOES NOT HAVE A STATE FRUIT)

USED IN: PIES JAMS SYRUP ICE CREAM

if you *like* THIS BOOK
TRY OTHER QUICK *facts*
BOOKS, AVAILABLE AT
THE COOLEST BOOK SHOPS
OR ONLINE.

9 798218 037758